Norman Dugdale was born in Bur
at Burnley Grammar School and Manchester University. He has lived in Belfast since 1948, where he worked as a civil servant until his retirement in 1984. From 1985 he has been a member of the board of the British Council and is chairman of the council's Northern Ireland Advisory Committee; he is also chairman of Bryson House.

Other poetry collections by Norman Dugdale:

Prospect of the West (Barrie and Jenkins, 1970)
Corncrake in October (Blackstaff Press, 1978)
Running Repairs (Blackstaff Press, 1983)

With every Good Wish!

Grenfell.

LIMBO

NORMAN DUGDALE

THE
BLACKSTAFF PRESS
BELFAST

First published in 1991 by
The Blackstaff Press Limited
3 Galway Park, Dundonald, Belfast BT16 0AN, Northern Ireland
with the assistance of
The Arts Council of Northern Ireland

Typeset by Textflow Services Limited

Printed by The Guernsey Press Company Limited

British Library Cataloguing in Publication Data
Dugdale, Norman
Limbo
1. English. Poetry
I. Title
821.914
ISBN 0-85640-468-3

for Mary

CONTENTS

Πάντα στὸν νοῦ σου νἄχεις τὴν Ἰθάκη.
Τὸ φθάσιμον ἐκεῖ εἶν' ὁ προορισμός σου.

Always you must have Ithaca in mind.
Arrival there is your predestined end.

from 'Ithaca' by Constantine Cavafy

SHROUDED COAST

Fend off those shades. They throng my dreams
With their high incessant chatter
Crowding round the trench or crouch like dogs
On all fours lapping up the blood.

It is not these that I would parley with,
But lost companions whose luck ran out:
Who even in the ribald fellowship
Of youth suddenly fell silent

Or vanished overboard without a cry
At midnight in mid-sea – pioneers
So far ahead I cannot read
Their signals now, much less interrogate

Them on this leafless, fog-bound shore.

DONEGAL

Look, this land, mist-shawled
Mostly, earth and sea and sky
A monochrome grey wash,
Is Midas-touched by spring,
Its ragged banks and boreens
Burgeoning gold: how soon spent
In wild profligacy of wind and rain.

ELDER STATESMAN

He was shopping, he said, leaning on his stick,
For his wife, who seldom ventured out these days.
I too had my instructions and a list
Of small necessities. We stood on the corner
While others – women mostly – hurried past,
Heads down, ignoring him, and talked of times gone by
And the evils fallen since upon the city:
Ancient codgers on the walls of Troy
Peering into the dust and smoke and din,
The confused carnage on the plain below.

ROBIN AMONG SUMMER VISITORS

Connoisseur of bread crumbs and grilled bacon rind,
He would materialise through fog and frost,
Wolf-light of the slinking dawn, with a sudden
Blink of wings outside the kitchen window,
Red kerchief slashed, pirate-fashion, round his neck.
A swivel of head and eye, a few brisk bobs,
And he was gone, to gorge or shelter God knows where.

Occasional accomplices apart – deft
Milk-bottle-raiding blue tits, the whole gang
Hooked on cream – he had the place all winter through
Almost to himself. Yet, so deafening the din
The squatters make these mornings crowded here
Within his tenement, he can't be seen
Or heard. Globetrotters, they will migrate with the sun

Soon enough. But will he swagger back then, buccaneer,
Chest puffed out, ready to defy the dark again?

NEW MANAGEMENT

The rooms were empty but the lights still on.
They had retouched the ceilings, moved the portraits round,
I noticed; but the tables, books, the leather chairs
And velvet draperies were much as I had found

Them years before – that slightly faded opulence,
The silence tingling with expectancy.
A woman entered whom I didn't know,
Sat behind the desk, and startled to see me,

'Yes?' she said. 'Can I help you?' 'Thank you,' I replied,
'I'm waiting for your colleague to appear,'
And mentioned the name. 'There must be some mistake,'
She said. 'There's nobody of that name here.'

'Nobody of that name here? Oh, come,' I said.
She bristled. 'Either you have picked the wrong address,
Or else this . . . this person that you speak of left
A long time since – under the old regime, I'd guess.'

'Old regime? What do you mean, the old regime?
And who are you?' I asked. 'Look. You'd better go,'
She said, and rang a bell. 'You weren't invited
And clearly you've no business here. This man will show –'

I'd turned already, blundering through the marble hall
And out. I had found the place again, no question,
Whatever that strange woman may have said:
But far too late – usurpers in possession,

The godhead overthrown, the sibyl fled.

SCHOOL PHOTOGRAPH

Head prefect, captain of the First XI,
He lounges there, athlete, aesthete, all the rage
In Wilde as wit, or Shakespeare as tragedian,
Presaging triumph on the West End stage,
And smiles into the future. Nathaniel
To his Berowne, gawky, shy,
Too easily put down, I recollect
Chiefly now his arrogance and vanity –
And seeing him later once on television
In a minor role, by younger men outshone.
He must be somewhere still, still craving stardom's call.

TRYST

Wind frets the low peninsula,
Scuffs pools, rubs cheekbones raw. Gulls screech,
Red-eyed, and squabble over small
Pickings on a bladderwrack-strewn shore

That shelves to mud. I crunch dry sticks
Along the strand, waiting for the faint
Susurrus in the distance, glint
And ripple of the tide that lifts

Stranded boats off their beam-ends,
Encircles islands, fills the creeks.
When will it fetch you shimmering in
To repossess your precincts,

Bring the bee-delighting scents
And stir of summer once again?

TYNAN

However slow its onset, catastrophe
Is always swift and ruthless at the last.
Night still, no stars; a sudden frenzied din,
Shrieking, sobbing, battery, conflagration,
Then silence: Troy, Mycenae, Tiryns dust

And rubble. O yes, it has happened before.
So, its harvest gathered, last thanksgiving said,
Long shadows of a late October sun
Wheeling across its lawns, this great house waited
For its end. Axes hacking down the door

That moonless night, shouts, shots, old man and his son
Dead in their blood, flames roaring through the roof –
All this was nothing new. The distant pyre
Signalled an ancient order's immolation,
The killers cockroaches scurrying from its glare.

LONG-DISTANCE COACH STATION

They fetch us back, familial errands,
Only to find how much we knew has changed.
I remember this soot-stained city, its grime
So deeply ingrained then that wind and rain

Could never scrub its stony visage clean.
Today its rectangles of shining glass and steel
Focus a fierce Italianate sun
Strayed somehow too far north. Passing through,

I pick my way by instinct more than knowledge
Down half-forgotten streets, past bare-legged girls
Cool in cotton, navvies stripped down to the waist,
To reach this stifling rendezvous, where I arrive

With hours to spare, and nothing to read or do
But wait for evening when the traffic melts
Towards cooling suburbs; and then last coaches come
Swinging in from London, Glasgow, Birmingham

With a blast of diesel fumes, a sudden cough
And spasm of engines spluttering to a stop.
Their passengers descend, are met with smiles,
Hugs, kisses, by mums, dads, husbands, boyfriends, wives,

Excited children; and, baggage seized, are whisked
To waiting cars that speed into the dusk.
I watch them go, who have no part in these
Small celebrations of love and joy

By strangers in a near-strange place. But that such rites
Are ageless is a consolation,
Let chance demit, time topple what it will.
Yes, even if (here's my lift now) those I attend

These days so rarely signify reunion,
So frequently farewell.

IN A LARGE GREEK COLONY: 200 BC

from Cavafy

That things aren't what they should be in the Colony
There remains not the slightest doubt. Possibly –
For all that we edge forward still somehow –
The time has come, as not a few think now,
To bring in a political reformer.

Yes. But the snag, the difficulty
Is that they make such a self-righteous fuss and stir,
These reformers, over every single thing.
(What a relief, what a blessing it would be
If they were never needed.) They pry
Into the smallest detail, prod and poke, essay,
And radical redispositions spring
At once to mind, to be pursued without delay.

Besides, they have a bent for sacrifice.
'Rid yourselves of that particular property.
Your occupation of it's insecure.
(Just such possessions undermine a colony.)
Abdicate your revenues from this
And from that other source. They're both impure.
Yes, and from this third, which follows naturally.
You need them, do you say? Don't be too sure.
They are a noxious responsibility.'

Then, as they prosecute their audit
They find more superfluities to cut –
Things hard for men, however, to forego.

And when, having finished at last, the whole show
Docketed in detail, all pared down to the bone,
They depart, taking the rewards that are their due,
We'll see what little's left, how small the residue
After such heroic surgery.

Well,
Perhaps the time hasn't yet quite come,
We mustn't panic. It is dangerous to rush.
Premature measures soon invite repentence. Sadly,
And certainly, much is wrong in the Colony.
But is there anything human free from blemish?
And after all, we do inch forward (don't we?) still.

INNER CITY

How it blows, skimming salt-marsh, slobland,
Green-ribbed rock, this bleak wind off the sea,
That rifles wharf and warehouse, splatters spray
On silent quays, rattles windows, smashes slates,
Rolls dustbins round back yards, lifts curtains, slams
Doors shut: blusters, sobs, blowing through the small

Moon-blanched hours like desolation
Through the derelict, depopulated
Wastes within where once were cafés, shops,
Couples sauntering beneath the lights
Of tree-lined avenues at dusk;
And in the suburbs only yesterday
New blossom, songburst, riot of the spring.

FINAL ACT

The game is up, the handcuffs on, stalls and pit
Await the curtain. What can he do but go
Quietly, this wild-eyed creature cornered so
Among his crimes? ('Come along, sir, now. We don't
Want to disturb the neighbours, do we, or
Frighten the kiddies at this hour of night?
Of course not, sir.') Yes, he's got his man, this gaunt
Black-booted emissary of the Law
Whose deadpan entrance always stops the show.

HALLOWE'EN

Beautiful pale girls whose copper hair
Cascades round their shoulders, trees in the park
Stand motionless at dusk. Far south-west the sun
Founders in a burst of sudden fire

That burnishes the city, then smoulders out.
In shops and offices the lights flick on
To ward off ghosts this night the earth exhales
Its dead, and spirits wander. I walk

Past disused bandstand, stripped flowerbed
In mist and silence here towards the gate
Where traffic churns, millracing through the falls
Beyond, and booming in the distance.

What if I should meet you even yet,
Walking towards me, smiling, summers since?

LOVERS

Deciphering the manuscripts exhumed
From centuries of dust and silence, scholars
Noted that her name, so vividly invoked
In the beginning, faded and then vanished
From later scrolls. Cooling passions, some estrangement,
A final rift that parted them for good?
So most commentators plausibly conjecture.
And yet it's possible, just possible
(Even against the odds such things can happen)
That they might have settled, the two of them,
For Roman domesticity: plump matron now
In middle age, paterfamilias weighed down
By paunch and jowl and gravitas. But then
One poem predicates she died still young and rose
From her ashes to taunt and haunt him. Well,
Who knows? Theses will be written yet,
Don will dispute with don. Early or late,
Together or alone, they ended, doubtless,
In a mess, shipwrecked like the rest of us.

HOMAGE TO THE BARD

Whose poems run straight
and thin as drainpipes
down the page, flushing
memories of the da,
dead in exile, and
the fiddle-playing uncle
who stored pikes in the thatch
at home, and helped the lads
send old Sir John's place up
one night in flames – only
nobody let on
then, you see, for fear
the peelers in
big shiny boots
would come and get them.
And it all slurps down, seeping
into the Great Bog
where the consciousness
of the race lies hidden
which the bovine Brits
and Prods, who don't belong,
can't find or fathom
ever, no matter how
they rampage round
and wreck the place. And Christ,
it's gloomy there
and rough as hell up here:
though sometimes
there's that girl again
with the wild dark eyes,

the lustrous hair
and delectable breasts
to take his mind off things.

CRETAN MANTINADA

Rank, riches, fame I never envied –
Only a limber frame, a cool, clear head.

AGE

Is crossing the Mall or Aldersgate
Before a wild stampede of traffic, mind
Signalling 'Move': only to find
You don't in fact accelerate.

PROGENY

His dreaming head, beached high and dry at dawn
Among the salt-bleached spars and bladderwrack,
Lifts, squinting at the whale-backed monsters torn
Through gates of ivory – or gates of horn.

TALKING HEAD

It isn't just what fills the frame or box –
The smile, the hairdo – that you ought to watch,
But mirthless eyes that give away the show,
The flick knife glinting in the fist below.

LEADER OF MEN

Strange how they foundered under him, each ship
In turn, all hands lost save one. As they sank
He bobbed up like a cork among the wreckage,
Gathering glory, medal ribbons, rank;
While in green darkness down below, his crews,
Open-mouthed but mute, rolled helpless at the news.

OLD MAN SITTING IN THE PARK

To renounce the world is one thing:
To be abandoned by it quite another.

NATURAL HISTORY

'The spiders hidden in high places here
Are weaving treason. We're flies caught in their trap,'
You cry. But then, they'd never cock things up
Like this, those subtle spinners you so fear.
No. When ignorance and folly squat
Like toads on top, arachnids scuttle clear.

TRADING STATION

Blown off course, storm-battered and leak-sprung,
He limped ashore in this Phoenician town
Whose quays and alleys teeming morning fills
With street cries, carts, swart foreign seamen jabbering
Among the bales and cordage: where heat bangs down
Like a dustbin lid at noon, clamping the din,
The sizzling flies, fish heads, straw, and smells
Of rotting fruit and garbage tight within.

Through the silence then of shuttered afternoon
Gold light filters onto golden skin
And shadowed eyes. He spends his manhood here
Whose business lies in distant waters, beached
In this creek of time, her salted mouth,
The scented whorls and sea-lift of her hair.

WHAT'S WRONG WITH ABERYSTWYTH?

'His first lectureship at Aberystwyth (about as inappropriate a place as possible) was followed . . . by a fellowship at Balliol.'

Book review in the *Spectator*

When she was twenty-one, Aunt Bertha –
Long before you were born, she used to say,
Spreading the tablecloth, her dimpled face
Beaming at her brother's three small children
(She would have given us anything
If ever she'd had anything to give
But hugs and smiles and home-made cake and jam) –
Went to Aberystwyth for a holiday.
She stayed there for a week in a boarding house
Just behind the seafront, the only time
She ever left home or was waited on.
And coming from the mills, the slag heaps, moors,
The cobbled streets and smoke-grained terraces
Of Lancashire, she thought the place was paradise.

PRE-RETIREMENT COURSE

Solon, the Athenian,
Gave himself, his life's work done,
To pleasures the prerogative
Of youth – wine, music, love;
And yet another handsome boy
Was Pindar's geriatric joy.

Pray, gentlemen, don't emulate
These carnal follies of the great
And good. They'd never do, such goings-on,
In Bath or Budleigh Salterton;
And think of the wagging hats, the shame
And outrage over tea in Cheltenham.

There's worse to come. You still can't live
Life backwards crowned with vine or olive –
No, not even in the bright Aegean.

THE COMMISSARS CONFIRM THEIR SHORT LIST

Yes, these are the big names. In their cots
They strangled snakes. Childhood and youth
Were full of portents; they came down
With Firsts in almost everything,
Famous already, then took the town
By storm. Yes, these are the big shots
Everybody's heard of. They will run –
Always to tumultuous applause –
A lyric sprint or prose-packed marathon
At the drop of a chequebook any day
In record time to grab the prize.
They're also good at gouging eyes
And kicking shins. (Why not, when they
Pick the ref and mostly write the laws?)

The rest are nameless, undefined
Except by what they're not: unplaced
Among the halt, the lame, the blind.
They'll never make the grand tour east
Of the Graeco-Roman cities, pack
The amphitheatre in Antioch
Or Ephesus. True, some might be sent
Where no one else will go – to Pontus,
Say, or Bactria maybe, where
They're glad of anybody, too uncouth
To notice lapses of deportment,
Unmodish manners, rustic training.
What might pass there would never do
For cultivated taste, or qualify

For Panhellenic sponsorship
Anywhere that matters . . .

Posterity?
Sod posterity. We shan't be here
When out of this whole rabblement
It disinters the real right thing.

AGE OF HEROES

O the afternoons of those wet Saturdays
In winter when we scuffled in the queue,
Then, slapping tuppence down, pushed and squeezed into
The tight-packed dark, ducking the missiles hurled
By rough boys at the back with gobstoppers
And bottles of exploding pop. How we'd cheer
And stamp when faithful Rin Tin Tin escaped at last
To warn his master, who, gun belt buckled on,
The deputy's tin star pinned on his chest,
Strode into the town's main street (suddenly
Unpeopled now) where bad men always bit the dust.

Childish, yes. But how many times since then
Have we stepped forth to knock some villain flat
In fantasy, with one contemptuous blow
Avenging private snub or public wrong –
The crowd acclaiming us, the hitherto
Far princess of our most lascivious dreams
Gasping her gratitude and admiration?
A pity life so rarely matches art:
That great Achilles broods still in his tent
Unrecognised, while boors and braggarts grab the spoils
Of Troy, the gorgeous diadems, the scented girls.

RIBBLESDALE

Like the flash of a kingfisher's wing
Skimming down some deep-shadowed stream
You dart into my memory, deft
And witty and delightful, a quick
Bright presence glimpsed again then gone.
No, not gone. Vivid, distant as a dream
The pebbled rivers, woods, the golden haze
Enfolding us that summer afternoon
We walked by Dinckley to Hurst Green.

ST JAMES'S, PICCADILLY

I

Wealth and fashion once adorned this church
For matings mostly, yes, but matins too,
Behind gloved hand or silken cuff and lace
Discreetly yawning through a Sunday sermon.

From elegant town house, from noble square,
Sinners of this parish everyone,
Or masters of many acres in the shires
And mistresses of country mansions come

With lady's maids and footmen, children, coachmen,
Cooks, to London for the season,
They entered here a rational universe
Of order, harmony, proportion

Grander by far than anything they knew
Yet still familiar: its lucid mystery
Prefigured in resplendent light,
Common day a sudden glory, golden, white.

II

Migrants seeking refuge from the roar
And gabble of a gross cosmopolis,
We flop down each in turn, two or three
Gathered together here in no one's name,

One resting old bones at the back, one
In seeming contemplation, a third in shorts

And open shirt, guidebook in hand, staring
At this late Carolingian masterpiece

Encased in sooty brick. Where have you absconded,
God? To what black hole beyond the galaxies,
What dim, deserted shrine where goat tracks cross
The mountain path, and snuffed cold candles splay,

And faded saints look down from flaking walls?
You give no sign. Incongruously lest
My steps disturb your silence, I tiptoe out,
One of the not-quite-unbelievers who

Drops small coins in the box beside the door
With the hollow clunk of metal upon wood
To ward off evil, assuage guilt; and so retreat
To the apophatic theology of the street.

MR CAVAFY'S BYZANTINE ARCHON VERSIFYING IN HIS EXILE

'Conventional stuff,' you say,
'Boring too – strict metre, rigid form,
Pompous, frigid as the man himself.'
Well, perhaps it kept the slinking wolf
That preyed on his small hours at bay,
This candle guttering through night and storm.

LAST NIGHT

Last night I saw you in my dreams again.
People were gathering, strangers mostly,
In some grand hall for cocktails before dinner,
Bejewelled, decorated, all in evening dress –
I among them, glass in hand, nodding, smiling,
Eyes ransacking the room for you in vain.

At table, then, one chair stood empty. At last
You came, charming the host with your apology
As you passed towards your place, your words
In that musical low voice I knew so well
Exciting laughter and applause. Avidly
I searched your face. You were hardly changed: no older
Certainly, more beautiful than ever,
Absorbed, it seemed, in conversation
With your attentive neighbours on each side.
Not knowing how to meet your gaze, I was afraid
That soon your glance might fall on me. But no.
You neither looked nor offered any sign
Of recognition, removed into a world
Not mine. I sat there, lips, mouth, dry, exalted
As always in your presence yet dismayed . . .

Then woke, shuffled round the bed, drew the curtains
Back. It was four o'clock: a long while before dawn.

MEDIZERS

They were rational men, the Medizers,
Not xenophobic or hysterical,
Their policy grounded firmly in self-interest –
To keep clear of a war they couldn't win
Against the Great King's overwhelming might
On land and sea. How could the Spartans, stubborn,
Arrogant as ever, hold Thermopylae
With a mere three hundred men and a rabble
Of helots and some half-trained hangers-on?
Athens too, all big talk since Marathon
And empty gestures – you'd see how soon her ships
Would cut and run for home when things got rough,
As they surely would, off Artemision.
There was no salvation from such quarters. No.
The one way of averting futile slaughter
Was to offer earth and water to the Mede
In token of submission, make a show
Of welcome, and save whatever could be saved
By bribery and diplomatic skill.

Thus
The Medizers, whom history consigned,
Knowing which side won, to obloquy.
They are still around today, realists
Counselling compromise and caution,
Men comfortably off with much to lose
Like their predecessors in that hot, dry spring.
Now, informed observers everywhere commend
Their moderation and good sense: not so

The creatures trapped here in the labyrinth,
Enemy or friend, who stumble through the common dark
Towards what glint of light, what sudden, squalid end?

CROSSINGS

It always started after dark, that journey,
Mostly in the dead of winter when
The boat train pulled out on its long haul north:
Slowed at last, jolting through junctions, clanked
And squealed then to a halt beside the quay
Past midnight, a keen wind whisking clouts of steam
Up beyond the lamplight. Stubbing cigarettes
Or yawning in the fug, the passengers
Struggled into coats, stuffed magazines away,
Reached luggage down, and stumbled out, straggling
Through muddy sheds towards the ship's black bulk
Bunched high above her moorings, the oily glint
Of sluggish water heaving in the dock.

The harbour lights recede, the last
Cold whimpers of a dying gale
Fret in the rigging. Against
Our rusty sides the flick and flash
Of a lighthouse beam through darkness
Swinging from unseen cliffs, the lift
And slap, hiss and slobber
Of the dream-tossed, paroxysmal sea,

The vessel booming, lurching through the night
Towards what landfall in the leaden murk
Of dawn, what gull-screams out of desolation?

Fitful sleep of slamming doors, sliding crates,
A drumming deck, woke to a horizon
Bleak enough: a long dark coast

Opening in the half-light massive jaws
Of black-fanged rock; then smudge of grey on either bow
Converging into mud banks, gantries, wharfs;
And cloaked in cloud, a raw and windy city
Raising blinds on puddled streets, another day.

This, then, is how it was, or seemed to be.
What rites of passage had we undergone?
What judgment, death, what strange rebirth?
How much was real, how much hallucination,
Or some kind of foreknowledge? We stepped ashore,
Each to his appointed end, head down,
Coat collar turned in the quotidian rain.

POLONIUS COMPLAINS

'he's for a jig or a tale of bawdry, or he sleeps'

It's not the spells of dullness or mere vacancy
That fret me most, dimmed sight, decay of powers.
At my age, one nods off all too easily.
No. It's the gabble of night voices in my head
Crackling through static: some mad insomniac
Who squats there in the dark, hours upon hours
Twiddling the wavebands of the set beside my bed.

SATAN'S ADVICE

Let it cohabit, this animal,
Together with the female of its kind
For weeks or months within a space confined
To them alone, called Paradise. They'll soon lust
For something new, surrounded by the dull
Scratched shards of boredom, bickering, disgust.

STAFF PARTY

She looked experienced as well as pretty.
I clowned a while and told my favourite jokes.
(One thing I said I really thought quite witty.)
She smiled, it's true, but didn't seem impressed
Till somebody mentioned Smyth. I pictured Smyth –
We all knew Smyth – him of the wheezy chest,
The woollen cardigan and grizzled head,
Old Granny Smyth, who never would
Be manager of this or any store.
'Oh, but I think he's wonderful,' she said,
Cheeks aglow, eyes shining. 'Tell me more.'

OLYMPIC GAMES

Afterwards, did he boast, say he was sorry
Like some, or simply withdraw without a word,
Leaving the girl to make up her own story
For scandalised ears, while back at home, bored
With the wife, he pictured how he would discharge
Himself on the next innocent at large?

APPARITION

'Fuckin' foreigner,' he said, his pale, mad face
Thrust into mine. 'Get to fuck out of Ulster.'
He had heard me exchange greetings – nothing more –
With an acquaintance passing in the street
Thronged with traffic: leapt forward and was gone,
Loping towards the Markets or Short Strand,
Before I could begin to gather myself.
Well over twice his age, I had lived here,
Worked here, longer by far than my assailant.
This was home . . .

And yet it was the sting
Of truth within his venom stopped me short.
For him and his kind I am the enemy
To be driven out, the scapegoat for all sins
Whose going will bring peace and brotherhood
Throughout the land. So they say, killing the while
Those they call their countrymen who happen still
To disagree.

What kinship can I claim
With the dissenters then? Another landscape,
Other weathers – mist and lough and mountain,
Drumlin, rock, the soughing rain – bent, moulded them
To psalm and Sabbath, field and byre and farmstead,
Clipped of speech, in a land of talkers taciturn
Keepers of counsel, cleaving to their gods.
A stubborn race, their virtues out of fashion,
Who will memorialise them now
That Hewitt's dead, and I a metic in their midst?

INSOMNIA

Last night I laid an ambush
To check your lodgement in my heart
And drive you from my head.
The poor ruse failed. Instead
You wound more deeply in my brain
And took possession of my heart
By right of conquest once again.
My love, why do you always thus
Invade each night my drunken heart
Yet still abjure my bed?

METAMORPHOSIS

vera incessu patuit dea

Tall, grey-eyed, she moved through summer with the lithe
Grace of an Athena in her elegant
Simplicity of sandalled foot and dress:
Then vanished, a remembered vision,

Only to reappear beneath the lamps
Of autumn, now with lipsticked mouth,
Blue-shadowed eyelids, hobble skirt and high
Black heels, her bangles, beads and earrings
Jingling like some tart's on a street corner
As she stepped out of the shadows, Aphrodite
Confronting my astounded gaze.

CELTIC BARD, BURGHER'S WIFE

Grizzled, broke, with a small child's grasping hands
And greedy mouth, he rolled his beer-blown gut
From pub to pub round Soho, from pub to party
At one of which they met. A plain Dutch mare
Turned skittish, she jumped her fences, fled the Netherlands
To join him for a passionate affair
In distant Ireland. But then unending rain,
Stale smells of cabbage lingering on stair
And corridor, a loudly creaking bed,
The landlady's cold sniff and shake of head
Fetched her in a few weeks home again
To level ways, those sober rich interiors
The Flemish masters knew. What next? That bird, maybe,
Above? The one in Barons Court? He's free
To prey once more for bed, booze, board: or worse,
He'll fornicate and multiply in verse.

REMORSE

Oh no: that it should come to this,
Such ruin, wrack, and bitterness
Between us two, all noxious, overgrown.
What serpent slid into our garden
With his false heart and subtle tongue
And curled about you with a hiss
And smile? So guileless they seemed then,
That smile, that kiss, how could you have known
They hid my crooked heart, my flickering tongue?

GEROUSIA

The first bright day of spring draws them out again,
Hobbling on their sticks into the park
To warm old bones, and watch excited dogs
And children chase each other across lawns.
It is colder than they think. The daffodils
Have not yet lifted, some of them, their heads
Even in this sun, but shiver in the wind
As these upon their benches now, huddled here
In coats and caps and scarves. 'Bit chilly still,'
I say, nodding as I pass. They grunt or nod
In turn, sparing speech. A year or two and I
Shall take my seat in their laconic council.

DOMESTIC INTERIOR

Winter kills them off, old dogs, old people,
Who once rebuffed its random malice
But have no stomach left now for a fight.
I wake, counting the chimes of a church steeple,
As usual at four, and blink to find
The room blanched with reflected light
Of newly fallen snow. A rising wind
Riffles through hedges as a conjurer
Riffles cards. Small creatures, birds and mice,
Snuggle against the cold as best they can.
Below, dog sprawled before a long-dead fire
Mumbles, stirs, slumps stiffly in his basket.
I pull the bedclothes round my neck. In heat
Of blood, shudder of tumescence, we began.

Beware the curse of general praise
That flatters, soon grows sated, then betrays
To contumely. Better by far endure
Neglect, whose stony places sometimes flower.

THE OTHER KINGDOM

Winter would be worst, I thought, its wild storms
Lashing your grave and beating down your flowers,
The byways blocked by snow, ice crusting ruts and mire,
Even your name, all that's still left of yours.
But I'd not bargained for your loveliness
In spring: primrose, daffodil and whin
A glory of sudden gold and green
In hedge, in hollow. To see you everywhere
Yet never to find you, this
Stabs the heart, is sharpest anguish.

ZOO

They screech and gibber, scutter, scratch and stink,
Kick, bite, claw for place and precedence
In snatching food or females; are groomed for fleas,
Assert their primacy with screams of rage.

It isn't mere hallucination
By hypoglycaemia induced or drink,
Nor yet the mordancy of shipwrecked age
That peoples streets with apes, baboons and monkeys

While gentle creatures languish in the cage.

WHITE CHURCH AT BALLINTOY

haec porta domini; justi intrabunt in eam

The village lines the coastal road, a thin
Straggle, Irish fashion, of houses, pubs,
Small shops, cottages: yet tidy, touched no doubt
By the Scottish passion for cleanliness
And order. A mile beyond, across broad fields
That slope towards the sea, the church stands on the edge
Of the escarpment, a solitary keep
In this treeless landscape tall, commanding
In the distance. But then, close by
It dwindles to squat tower, blunt nave,
Its whitewash flaked blue-grey, a low stone wall
Crooked around its dead, in hummocked earth
Patiently awaiting resurrection.

I try the door, which yields, and entering find
All seemly, plain within, quite unmistakeably
Anglican in the Hibernian mode
Outcropped here among the deep
Striated seams that riddle this rock-bound coast,
The world's end once, whose massive boreal headlands
Rebuff the North Atlantic's fling and fury.
But not today. Today a slumbering sea
Nuzzles the tiny harbour down below.
Due north, Islay and the Paps of Jura
Smudge the far horizon, which kindles briefly now
Far in the west, then smoulders like snuffed wick. Fleeting
As a gull's faint cry that fades into the dusk
Across these great grey waters, the hungers

Here of flesh, blood's fever, heart's delirium
Are gathered into solitude and silence
With all the generations gone before.

In the decaying light of late November
I have come here craving commerce with the dead.
Along the empty pews my footsteps echo
Hollowly on wood. Not meaning to, I sink
On stiff and unaccustomed knees, old man,
Who finds no words that can articulate,
Or prayer appease, the dog's howl of his grief.

LIMBO

The track ends here in reeds, and fog
And silence. Nothing stirs.
There is no way forward, no way back:
Nothing to do but wait, to listen

For muffled voices, the creak
And splash of oars, a keel
Grating on shingle. Or possibly
Tomorrow or the next day, or the next

Again, the wind may rise, cleansing
Vision for a moment to reveal
A foundered sun, gouting smoke and fire
Beyond the desolate horizon

And on the far shore mud banks, marshland, dull
Miasma of corruption and despair.

While some of the poems in this collection have appeared before, almost all are now published for the first time. With one or two exceptions of much earlier origin, they belong to the last few years.

page 11 — 'In a large Greek colony: 200 BC'. Cavafy's translators rarely attempt to reproduce his rhymes, presumably because they are so difficult to carry over into English without disrupting his rhythm or distorting his tone. John Mavrogordato is the exception that proves the rule. His unrhymed versions of Cavafy are among the most accomplished I know; but when he rhymes, he does so with an exuberance quite out of keeping with Cavafy's habitual restraint and gravity of address. Cavafy is supremely a poet of statement and irony, not of vivid image or arresting metaphor. (In this respect he fails to conform to contemporary Western notions of what poetry should be.) His rhymes are exact but unobtrusive, reinforcing meaning without drawing attention to technique. It is, of course, impossible fully to reflect in English either Cavafy's inimitable voice or his versification, much less to echo his multiple ironies. Nevertheless, rhyme is an important part of his armoury, not to be ignored. Unemphatic devices, such as pararhyme, near rhyme, rhyming on final *y* to mimic Cavafy's frequent rhymes on unstressed *ee*, are, it seems to me, legitimate means of approximating his effects.

page 19 'Cretan mantinada': the mantinada is a traditional verse form in the island of Crete, consisting of a rhymed couplet, often, but not always, with satiric intent.

page 37 'Medizers': Greeks who sided with the Persians (Medes) when Xerxes, the Persian king, invaded Greece with massive force in 480 BC.

page 50 'Gerousia': the council of elders at Sparta which had large jurisdiction in political affairs and formed the highest executive committee of the state.

OTHER POETRY TITLES

from

THE BLACKSTAFF PRESS

AFTER SEYMOUR'S FUNERAL

ROY MCFADDEN

They tidy papers, retrospectively
Put lives in order. I have made out Herbertson's will,
Spoken of books to Mullan. Monaghan
Has named a college for his manuscripts.
They are busy editing their yesterdays,
Tailoring tall tales for mythology.
I watch their evening stumble into night.

from 'After Seymour's funeral'

Always notable for a certain elegant precision, Roy McFadden's poetry has drawn much of its strength from his obdurate refusal to revere the sacred cows of political and literary life.

In these latest poems, he rejects the mere 'editing of yesterdays' for a painstaking audit, accurately balancing the exaltations and discomfitures of youth against the wry self-knowledge of maturity. The result is writing of the highest order: elegiac, controlled and profoundly personal.

'McFadden remains at all times open-eyed, if seldom wide-eyed . . . a watchful presence, perceptive and unblinkered.'
Aidan Carl Mathews, *Irish Press*

198 x 129 mm; 80 pp; 0 85640 434 9; pb
£5.95

DADDY, DADDY

PAUL DURCAN

WHITBREAD POETRY WINNER 1990

'A startling, funny, critical and mesmerising book of verse, one of the most purely enjoyable collections I've read for years . . . *Daddy, Daddy* is a candid, subtle, daring book. And painfully funny.'
Brendan Kennelly, *Irish Times*

'Its triumph . . . is to preserve all of Durcan's satirical brio while projecting it on to an inner landscape of love, solitude, domestic affections.'
Terry Eagleton, *Independent on Sunday*

'Like Sylvia Plath's *Daddy*, Durcan's father is often a terrifying figure of savage vindictiveness; at the same time, Durcan expresses for him a child-like and simple tenderness. Their relationship is imagined at various times in different guises – as father, lover, brother, wife – and the effect of this is an unsettlingly comical candour.'
Andrew Swarbrick, *Oxford Times*

'This new work is bursting with variety and strength.'
Dermot Bolger, *Sunday Press*

'For him poetry is story-telling and his stories are told in a direct fashion that makes them totally accessible . . . Paul's poetry sings, it moves the reader with its bareness.'
Roger McGough

Shortlisted for the 1990 *Irish Times*/Aer Lingus Irish Poetry Prize

198 x 129 mm; 208 pp; 0 85640 446 2; pb
£5.95

THE SELECTED PAUL DURCAN

edited by

EDNA LONGLEY

Provocative, inventive, controversial, Paul Durcan is one of Ireland's best-loved and best-selling poets. His work is a heady blend of intense lyricism and razor-sharp satire, moving urgently from tender love poetry to passionate attacks on political and spiritual corruption. Shining through it all is his unique personal vision of the modern world, uncompromising but profoundly life-enhancing.

CRITICAL ACCLAIM FOR PAUL DURCAN

'writes to the utmost limits of integrity and truth to capture the core of Ireland'
Martin Booth, *Tribune*

'His poetry speaks with a universal voice that touches people, irrespective of class, race or age, as witnessed by anybody who has heard Durcan read in public.'
Aidan Murphy, *Sunday Press*

'an unusual gift of empathy towards those whose lives he glimpses in passing and transforms into fictional surreal truth'
Harriet Waugh, *Spectator*

'probably the most completely original voice in Irish poetry'
Brendan Kennelly

198 x 129 mm; 144 pp; 0 85640 354 7; pb
£5.95

POETS FROM THE NORTH OF IRELAND

edited by

FRANK ORMSBY

POETRY BOOK SOCIETY RECOMMENDATION 1991

A splendid new edition – completely revised and updated – of Frank Ormsby's definitive anthology of Northern Irish poetry.

This new edition of Frank Ormsby's acclaimed anthology is a completely revised and updated selection presenting a comprehensive spectrum of twentieth-century Northern Irish poetry – from the restlessly contemplative poetry of John Hewitt to the highly crafted and personal work of Seamus Heaney. Here also is the wit and invention of Paul Muldoon; Michael Longley's brilliantly allusive poems; and Padraic Fiacc's nightmare vision of Belfast.

With revised selections from poets as widely diverse as Roy McFadden, Seamus Deane and Ciaran Carson, this new edition also includes ground-breaking work from the new generation of poets who have emerged since the first edition in 1979 – poets like Medbh McGuckian and Robert Johnstone – making this an authoritative and indispensable introduction to Northern Irish poetry.

210 x 148 mm; 352 pp; 0 85640 444 6; pb

£9.95

THE LONG EMBRACE

TWENTIETH-CENTURY IRISH LOVE POEMS

edited by

FRANK ORMSBY

Tender, passionate, bitter, bawdy, reverential – the poetry of love in Ireland is as various as the lovers and the poets. This anthology presents the best Irish love poems of the twentieth century. Some are uninhibitedly direct, others careful and emotionally circumspect, but together they display the sturdiness, the fragility, the transforming power of love in its everyday, familiar settings and circumstances: love as it flourishes – or fails to flourish – in youth and old age, inside and outside marriage; love as sharing of caresses, love ending in blows; love in time of war; love as it is trammelled by and defies the puritanical dictates of church and state.

Vigorously colloquial or musically formal, rich in imagery or quietly restrained, these poems, selected by the Irish poet Frank Ormsby,
'. . . record love's mystery without claptrap,
Snatch out of time the passionate transitory.'

'a very lively and accomplished collection'
Times Literary Supplement

'Every faithful spouse, every licentious rake, every heart-smitten or heart-broken lover should have a copy, preferably on the bedside locker.'
Irish Times

198 x 129 mm; 208 pp; 0 85640 387 3; pb
£7.95

TRIO POETRY 6

ANGELA GREENE, OLIVER MARSHALL,
PATRICK RAMSEY

Continuing Blackstaff's ground-breaking *Trio* series, this new poetry anthology presents the innovative work of three emerging Irish talents.

Angela Greene's powerfully visualised poems range from intricate studies of family life to work of intense lyricism. And through the vitality of their lucid domestic imagery, these poems confront death and loss. Breaking down the artificial division between the mundane and the visionary, the rich expression of her poetry is full of unexpected delights.

Oliver Marshall's carefully crafted work is by turns poignant and amusing. Exhibiting a sharp relish of words, the novel language of these poems is drawn from an eclectic range of sources – classical music, Christianity, European languages, Irish place names – and employed with unerring exactness. Whether surveying his immediate domain or tackling larger questions of faith and doubt, Marshall displays a sensibility that is both Irish and European.

Patrick Ramsey exercises a watchful and meticulous control of his subject matter. Firmly rooted in the landscape of Belfast, his poems evoke a powerful sense of place, and in his diffident, gentle love poems, Ramsey's attention to the fine details of 'the ordinary' touches upon the emotions lying within silence.

198 x 129 mm; 80 pp; 0 85640 431 4; pb
£5.95

ORDERING BLACKSTAFF BOOKS

All Blackstaff Press books are available through bookshops. In the case of difficulty, however, orders can be made directly to the publisher. Indicate clearly the title and number of copies required and send order with your name and address to:

CASH SALES

Blackstaff Press Limited
3 Galway Park
Dundonald
Belfast BT16 0AN
Northern Ireland

Please enclose a remittance to the value of the cover price plus: £1.00 for the first book plus 60p per copy for each additional book ordered to cover postage and packing. Payment should be made in sterling by UK personal cheque, postal order, sterling draft or international money order, made payable to Blackstaff Press Limited.

Applicable only in the UK and Republic of Ireland
Full catalogue available on request